TAE

ACKNOWLEDGMENTS
DEDICATION
INTRODUCTION

CHAPTER 1	He Is Present	1
CHAPTER 2	The Goodness of God	7
CHAPTER 3	Don't Move My Bed	11
CHAPTER 4	Runaway Bunny	17
CHAPTER 5	Trust and My Inner Control Freak	21
CHAPTER 6	Anger Awakened	29
CHAPTER 7	But What about My Pillowcase?	35
CHAPTER 8	Inadequate	41
CHAPTER 9	It's Not about Me	45
CHAPTER 10	Peel Away	51
CHAPTER 11	A Boy's Broken Heart	55
CHAPTER 12	Desire to Be Close	61
CHAPTER 13	Milk for the Soul	69
CHAPTER 14	Obedience Is Better than Sacrifice	73
CHAPTER 15	Mama's Armor	79
CHAPTER 16	This Little Light of Mine	85

ABOUT THE AUTHOR

ACKNOWLEDGMENTS

First and foremost, I thank God, my Creator, for giving me this desire to write, and for using me to encourage others.

My parents, who have shown me the love of Jesus, day in and day out. They are my example and my support, and because of them, I am fulfilling my dreams.

My husband, Stefan, my partner in this beautiful life with three boys. For being a man of God that these little boys can look up to.

DEDICATION

For Zachary, Gavin, and Lincoln.

I love you, a bushel and a peck.

INTRODUCTION

In our everyday grind, it is easy to get discouraged. We encounter feelings of frustration, heartache, anger, fear, and hopelessness. As parents, we can feel all of those emotions within five minutes, making it easy to get lost in the lie that we aren't loved and that we don't matter to God.

In this book, I will show you how God uses my role as a mom to teach me about His character. I will share how He has opened my eyes to see Him in everyday moments. I know your time is precious, and it feels like you don't have five extra minutes, but you will be able to open this book and find hope, encouragement, and perspective in just a few minutes. I am giving you sixteen examples of how God has worked in my life and shown me how He cares for me. In just a few minutes, you can learn more about who God is and have a great picture of how God sees you.

As a mom to three little boys, I probably don't have to tell you that my faith is tested every day. I am by no means a parenting expert, but I am a real person. I struggle with anger, impatience, control, and fear, but I believe that God is great at using the hopeless to show others hope. He has given me a gift to see Him in the everyday. Since becoming a parent, I feel like my heart has been opened to see who He truly is.

After reading this book, I pray you will also have your heart opened to see what God has to tell you. In just a few moments, you will feel inspired by the experiences that I have had, and you will want to draw nearer to God.

I believe that God will use this book to speak to you, in your own life. People say that God doesn't speak directly to us, but I know that if you want to hear what God is saying to you, all you have to do is ask. He can use anyone, or any experience, to show you who He is. It only takes a moment to change your perspective.

If you would take just a few minutes every day to hear a message God has for you, I promise you will be changed. Sometimes all we need is to hear that someone else is fighting the same battles. Finding hope and support can be the difference between living a fearful life and a joyful one.

There are always excuses: I don't have time. I am too tired. God doesn't care about my day-to-day life. Don't let the lies of the enemy defeat you.

Dear friend, find the hope and joy that God has called you to today. Pick up this book and start finding the truth about who God is and how He feels about you.

CHAPTER 1

He Is Present

Where can I go from your Spirit?
Where can I flee from your presence?
If I go up to the heavens, you are there;
if I make my bed in the depths, you are there.
If I rise on the wings of the dawn,
if I settle on the far side of the sea,
even there your hand will guide me,
your right hand will hold me fast.
If I say, "Surely the darkness will hide me
and the light become night around me,"
even the darkness will not be dark to you;
the night will shine like the day,
for darkness is as light to you. ~Psalm 139: 7-12

I am not a morning person, but having children has placed me in the early part of the day, the part where light breaks through the remaining darkness of the night. Warmth replaces cold. Stirring and life fill the stillness, the quiet.

In these moments—in the moments I did not plan and perhaps even resisted—God is here, in the joy in the baby's giggles, in the peace in the silent house. His presence fills each part. Each of these unplanned opportunities that parenthood places upon me promises His plan.

As with everything in life, love is a choice. Choosing to be light instead of darkness, picking peace rather than restlessness, navigating these rough waters of raising children ... I cannot do any of it alone.

My God is with me, even in moments of mayhem. Maybe I don't always see it that way; it can be difficult when disorder rules the day. Feeling calm in the frustration does not come naturally. But ...

He is there in the 3:00 a.m. feedings.
He is there in the scraped knees.
He is present in the piles of toys and dirty laundry.
He is present in the school pickup line.
He sees the tears, mine and theirs.
He sees each sacrifice and labor.
He hears each plea for patience.

He hears every shout of victory.
He feels my heart's cry for their salvation.
He feels my joy in their kisses.

Sweet cheeks, loud yells, filthy hands ... He sees, hears, feels all, and He is there.

What I have to remember is that I need not go far to find Him. When it appears there is nothing but adversity, when I feel lost at each turn, I know He is there in the thick of it all, quietly molding my heart into His.

These three boys I have, they are my heart. They belong to me. There is a fierce, deep sense of ownership that comes from being their mother.

I felt that way when each of them were born, most recently with Lincoln. My pregnancy with him seemed to go on ... and on ... and ON. I spent so much of that time waiting for him, longing to meet him. I fought and endured and labored to get him here. I carried him with me and knew him before he made his entrance into the outside world.

Once he finally arrived, there was no joy like it. I held him, and we looked into each other's eyes. I knew him, and he knew me. It was love before first sight, confirmed in that first gaze. Somehow he wasn't just a newborn; our souls connected as mother and son. It was like he knew what I had gone through, and I knew his heart, all in those few seconds. I felt relief and joy. I felt complete.

I have no doubt that God was with us in that moment.

If I, an imperfect human, am capable of this kind of love, how can I doubt that God loves me?

There is nothing my children could do to make me love them any less. Could they disappoint me? Yes. Could they hurt me? Unfortunately, yes. I have a tender heart, and that first time I heard one of them say he didn't love me ... it pierced me deeply. I knew he didn't mean it, but hearing those words was still painful. Even when they disobey, I still love them. I don't like their actions, but I still love *them*.

I am not a perfect parent (not even close). But if I take the things that are true about me as a parent and how I feel toward my children, I can get a better understanding and perspective of how God thinks of me, as his daughter.

I am His. I belong to Him. He created me. He chose to create me, wanted to create me.

For you created my inmost being;
you knit me together in my mother's womb.
I praise you because I am fearfully and wonderfully made;

... Your eyes saw my unformed body;
all the days ordained for me were written in your book before one of them came to be. ~Psalm 139:13, 16

He has a plan in this chaos called parenthood, teaching me in each trial, softly whispering His affections each morning. Even if I can't see it, He draws me closer with each breath.

Never will I leave you; never will I forsake you.
~Hebrews 13:5

No matter what the cost, He loves us anyway. He loves me in my disobedience, in my repetitive, redundant, recurring sins. He forgives me every time. There is nothing I can do to make him love me less, and there is nothing I can do to make Him love me more. He loves us all the while.

Consider the ravens: They do not sow or reap, they have no storeroom or barn; yet God feeds them. And how much more valuable you are than birds! ~Luke 12:24

His presence is always there. I just have to choose to see it. I can see Him in the everyday, if I invite Him in. Lord, live in these moments with my littles, and surround us with Your presence.

CHAPTER 2

The Goodness of God

I remain confident of this: I will see the goodness of the Lord in the land of the living. ~Psalm 27:13

Lately, I have been thinking about and dwelling on God's character. A few attributes have stood out to me, one of them being His goodness. What does that really mean? What does that look like? How do I see God's goodness in this harsh world?

I teach my children so many things, everything from walking and talking to manners and baseball. My role is to teach, to guide, to discipline. I encourage them and love them. I nurture them and take care of them. I feed them, clothe them, and provide for them. I show them right from wrong and how to be functional, productive people. I knew this was my job as a parent before I became one. What I never expected was for them to teach me.

Each one of my boys is special, unique, and precious to me. They each have their own personalities, their own strengths and weaknesses. There are things that I see in them, the good things, that I know are a direct reflection of God. We are created in His image, right? If we let Him, God can shine right through us.

Gavin, my middle boy, my sweetheart, as I call him, is an open book. All it takes is one look at his little face, and you can usually tell what he is feeling. If you are not sure, you won't have to wait long to find out because he also tells you everything you want (and don't want) to know. He is very passionate. With that passion can come some challenges, but most of the time he uses it for good.

When I look for God's goodness in this world, I see it in Gavin. I do not mean he is perfect, but I feel like God is using Gavin to teach me about Himself.

One of my favorite things about Gavin is his generous spirit. He gives so freely; he shares everything with others. He was given new Play-Doh for Christmas, and since he knew that Zachary, my oldest son, did not get any, he gave some to him—no strings, no hesitation. He just wanted to make Zachary happy. Whenever I give him a treat like Skittles or some chocolate, he picks out my favorite color or kind and gives it to me. I gave him a snack size Kit Kat, and he gave half of it to me. He even acts offended if you don't accept it.

He also shares his heart freely, and he feels deeply. When he heard a song I was listening to in the car, he said, "Mom, that song makes me cry for happy." He frequently gives me hugs and kisses, just because. When I say his name in a certain tone, he says, "I know, Mom. I love you too."

Gavin remembers when I have mentioned people who are sick, or who need our prayers. He reminds me to pray for them, or he tells me that he prayed for me three times today. He truly cares for others and their well-being. If someone is hurt, or if someone is being left out, he sees that. I have found him actually encouraging ME, trying to make my day better. My kid, my four-year-old, takes care of me. It is humbling, to say the least. He is kind, forgiving, and helpful.

I say all of these things not to praise Gavin, but to praise his Creator. I know that the good I see in Gavin is straight from the Lord. The best parts of him are a reflection of his Maker.

I feel like because there is so much focus on negative things in this world that I forget to stop and see God's goodness. I believe God gave me the children He did for a reason; He had a purpose in mind when He made me their mother. I believe that one purpose he has for me, as their mother, is to raise godly men to go out and love, protect, and give to this world.

Again, what I didn't realize, is how they would strengthen me. God knows my heart, and He knows that I need kind words and encouragement. He knows I need to feel loved. I know that God uses Gavin, daily, to show me those things.

Every hug, smile, or red Skittle is a little gift from God to show me His goodness. He reminds me that He loves me and that He is worthy of worship. Not because of these little gifts, no. Because of who He is, I fall down before Him.

*Come, let us bow down in worship,
let us kneel before the Lord our Maker;
for He is our God.* ~Psalm 95:6-7a

I look at my son, and my heart is full of the goodness of God.

I encourage you to look for the goodness of God in your own children. See Him in them. Open your heart and see how God can speak to you, through your own kids. Don't be so fixated on teaching them that you miss the things God can teach you.

*I myself am convinced, my brothers and sisters, that you yourselves are full of goodness, filled with knowledge and competent to instruct one another.
~Romans 15:14*

CHAPTER 3

Don't Move My Bed

I the Lord do not change. ~Malachi 3:6

My oldest son, Zachary, absolutely hates it when I change things. It could be changing his routine, getting the wrong snack, or worst of all—moving his bed.

I know that children like routine and some get upset if you change it on them, but I never thought that the simple act of turning the direction of a twin bed would bring about the end of the world. Every time I need to rearrange furniture in my six- and four-year-old's room, it causes devastation.

Gavin is fine with it. In fact, he usually compliments me on how nice it looks. But oh ... Zachary. It is just too much for him to take. He panics, gets angry, and has even cried. Eventually he gets over it—maybe even deciding that he likes it better that way—but for a week at least, he tells me how much he can't stand it.

I think, *Come on ... seriously? It's just a bed. It will be fine. It is not a big deal! Why is he freaking out over this? Is it just because it is change?*

Then, it happened.

I was at work, having a discussion with my boss, and she unexpectedly informed me that I would be doing something different and—not only that—I would be moved to a different team. Do you know what I did?

I panicked. I got angry. I totally cried.

There I was, thinking for several hours that I was witnessing Armageddon. I stewed, I cried a little more, I got very angry. It wasn't until later that night—or even the next morning—that I found peace with it.

I had to tell my friend, my coworker, what was happening because I knew she would be just as upset as I was. But as I was explaining it to her, it came over me ... *this really isn't that bad*. Then the more I thought about it, and the more I talked about it, I realized that it could turn out to be a really good thing, for both me and my friend. I thought, *Why did this upset me so much?*

I couldn't figure it out. Then ...

Lightbulb.

It was change. It was different.

Now I know how Zachary feels, and I know where Zachary gets it. I might as well have yelled at my boss, "Don't move my bed!!!"

It made me start to think about and to dig down to understand why change is so hard.

It's uncomfortable.
It's unpredictable.
It's different.
I want to control things myself.
I hate it just because it's change.

When I look at these things, I know that is what Zachary hates about it too.

I feel I am an optimistic person; I see the good in people and in situations, but it's easier for me to see those things for others. It's harder when it is myself, or my own situation. So on that note, why is change good?

I learn.
I grow.
I might do things I never expected.
It challenges me
It might be better.
It fights complacency.

If one thing is consistent about my life, it is that things are always changing. I think the uncertainty, the fear, is the hardest to overcome. In every situation, no matter what is changing, there is One that never changes. He always stays the same.

Faithful.
Loving.

Mighty.
Peaceful.
Holy.

Even when things get rearranged, or taken away, or aren't as I expected, there is one place to plant my feet, one place to go. I cling to the unchanging God. I set my feet upon the Rock. I look in His Word and see His promises.

*No one will be able to stand against you all the days of your life. As I was with Moses, so I will be with you; I will **never leave you nor forsake you.** ~Joshua 1:5*

*Cast all your anxiety on him because **he cares for you.** ~1 Peter 5:7*

The disciples went and woke him, saying, "Master, Master, we're going to drown!"
He got up and rebuked the wind and the raging waters; the storm subsided, and all was calm. ~Luke 8:24

I let the storms blow and the rain fall, but I look to my Jesus and wait for Him to calm the storm. Change will come, but when it does, my house is built on the Rock and will never be shaken.

Therefore everyone who hears these words of mine and puts them into practice is like a wise man who built his house on the rock. The rain came down, the streams rose, and the winds blew and beat against that house; yet it did not fall, because it had its foundation on the rock. ~Matthew 7:25-25

Now I just need to share that with my six-year-old and show him where to plant his feet ... right alongside mine.

CHAPTER 4

Runaway Bunny

God's kindness is intended to lead you to repentance.
~Romans 2:4

One of Gavin's favorite books for me to read to him is *Runaway Bunny* by Margaret Wise Brown. There are a few books he always wants me to read, but this one is one of my favorites too. Gavin likes to pick stories where he can curl up with me so that we can enjoy them together. (If you haven't read it, I definitely recommend it.)

In the story, the little bunny talks about how he wants to run away from his mama, and to where he will run. Each time the little bunny mentions where he will run, the mama bunny says she will be wherever he is, and she will find him.

After the little bunny exhausts his list of places he can run, he finally decides to stay where he is and to belong to his mama.

I love the picture this story paints. The little bunny learns how much his mama loves him and that she will be there for him, no matter what lengths she has to go to.

But what is it about the mama bunny that makes the little bunny realize he wants to stop running? He sees that wherever he runs, she will be there. Her kindness and who she is makes him desire to be with her, and to belong to her.

As I was reading it the other night, it called to mind one of my most cherished verses:

For I am convinced that neither death nor life, neither angels nor demons, neither the present nor the future, nor any powers, neither height nor depth, nor anything else in all creation, will be able to separate us from the love of God that is in Christ Jesus our Lord.
~Romans 8:38-39

I reflected on that verse and on the story I had just read. Truly, Jesus loves me so much that nothing can separate me from Him. Look at what Jesus went through to allow me to be with Him forever. He endured the cross and death, and He conquered hell to bring me home to Him.

In my own running from God, what brings me to repentance? What makes me change my mind and turn from my sin? I see my own deficiencies, my need for God. I see that I can't do it on my own; I can't save myself. Maybe I see the pain that it causes God when I sin, when I offend Him. The Holy Spirit calls me and draws me in.

What is it about God that draws me in? It is who He is. I am captivated by His kindness. I choose Him because nothing else compares. His grace is irresistible.

Romans 2:4 says, "God's kindness is intended to lead you to repentance."

When I hear that phrase, it truly turns things a little upside down for me. As parents, we have tried to be strict and discipline our children. If they disobey, there are consequences. Teaching children right from wrong and how to make the right choices usually involves them wanting to avoid some sort of punishment.

I do believe discipline is necessary and that it is the right thing to do. However, when I am teaching my children, what is going to stick with them? Are they obeying out of fear of negative consequences, or because they know our intentions for them are good and they trust us? It is a combination of both, but it is really about the attitude of the heart. Do they see their wrong behavior, and does it sadden them, causing them to consciously change their mind because they know who God is? We should be changed by God's kindness. If we genuinely see WHO God is, we want to stop running because we've found what we are looking for.

What is my reaction to God's grace? To His gifts that I do not deserve? I want to follow Him. I want to sit with Him, secure in the kindness of my Savior, with no desire to be anywhere else.

God wants to show me His love and His desire for me to be with Him.

For God so loved the world that he gave his one and only Son, that whoever believes in him shall not perish but have eternal life. ~John 3:16

So I will just stay here and belong to Him. I will be His "little bunny."

CHAPTER 5

Trust and My Inner Control Freak

In him at all times, you people; pour out your hearts to him, for God is our refuge. ~Psalm 62:8

I'm a pretty relaxed person.

At least I was before becoming a parent. Or maybe I just thought I was.

I'm not quite sure what it is, but becoming a parent has shown me that I am, in fact, a control freak. Maybe not in every aspect of my life, but when it comes to things with my children, I have found that I tend to try to control it all:

- What they wear
- What toys they have
- How their toys are organized
- Their schedules
- How situations will play out
- How they perform tasks
- Etc., etc., etc.

Perhaps this is just a "mom thing," but I know that some of it is just because I want things the way I want them. With other things, like schedules and situations, things have gone south in the past, so I try to do everything I can to prevent that from happening again.

For example, I hate to feel rushed. It stresses me out and turns me into a tornado of yelling, panicking, and grabbing. So when I have somewhere to be and a lot of preparation needs to be done, I've been known to plan out my day to the minute. (This mostly occurs when planning around a nursing baby because the timeline is crucial.) I hate to be running around last minute, trying to grab the things we need or yelling at everyone to find their shoes. Planning ahead is a good thing, and being prepared isn't a bad idea. However, when things don't go exactly according to plan, I tend to get angry or upset. Enter yelling-panicking-grabbing-tornado-mom.

Planning what clothes or shoes the boys wear or what toys they get for their birthday ... those things are not really important, but I like to control them anyway, and once I started on this control-freak path, it started to bleed into the other aspects of my life and ... well, control it. I want to control everything.

Where does this need to control everything come from?

It boils down to one thing: fear.

The fear that things are not going to turn out like I wanted or planned.
The fear that I won't like it, or that it will be painful.

The fear that something else or someone else is dictating my actions.

When I break it down even further, it translates into a lack of trust in God.

What is trust? It's a reliance on the integrity, strength, ability, and surety in someone/something else.

When I give my boys instructions to do something, I have a purpose for doing that. Do they trust that I want good things for them? Do they trust that I know what is best for them? Do they trust me to keep them safe, and that I will keep my word? The key to their obedience is rooted in their trust in me. If they believe that their way is better or that I don't have their best interest at heart, will they have a desire to obey?

My desire to control everything and to have things my way is really not any different from that of a six-year-old.

My trust in God needs to be based on the knowledge of who He is. He is my Creator, the designer of my soul, the author of my heart. Who better to know what I need than Him? The foundation of my trust is knowing His character.

God is:

Love

And so we know and rely on the love God has for us. God is love. Whoever lives in love lives in God, and God in them. ~1 John 4:16

Merciful

But in your great mercy you did not put an end to them or abandon them, for you are a gracious and merciful God. ~Nehemiah 9:31

Righteous

You are righteous, Lord, and your laws are right. ~Psalm 119:137

Holy

And they were calling to one another: "Holy, holy, holy is the Lord Almighty; the whole earth is full of his glory." ~Isaiah 6:3

Compassionate, Faithful

Because of the Lord's great love we are not consumed, for his compassions never fail.
They are new every morning;
great is your faithfulness. ~Lamentations 3:22-23

If I know these things and recognize who God is, that tells me what He wants for me. He knows what is best for me. If I know this, then why do I fight so hard to have my own way?

It is a constant battle of the flesh versus the spirit. My sinful flesh wants the control, and it fights tooth and nail against the spirit. This is the story of our life here on earth, waging war against the flesh. The good news is that we don't have to do this on our own. As a follower of Jesus, the Holy Spirit is with us, teaching us, comforting us.

Now that I know trying to control it all comes from a place of fear and flesh, what can I do to change it?

The more I become familiar with who He is, the easier it will be to let go. Isn't it easier to trust those we know and love than it is a stranger? Would I put my life in the hands of someone I barely know or with someone who cares for me? If I know someone's character and behaviors, I know if I trust them or not.

When I start to stress about every detail, I should spend time in the Word and rest in His promises. When I get angry that things haven't gone according to plan, I should step back and whisper my fears to Him so that He can calm my trembling heart. When I worry that things will not turn out, I should remember all the times He has provided for me in the past.

After we found our current church, I was meeting weekly with another mom. She reached out to me, took me in, and helped me set my eyes on Jesus. In one of our get-togethers, amidst my tears of frustration and fear of a situation, she simply asked, "When hasn't He taken care of you?"

I go back to that question a lot. It's so basic, but oh, so true. When I get anxious that things are not going my way, I take a step back and think through ALL that the Lord has brought me through so far. Knowing what He has done and how He has provided in the past gives me clear reasons to trust Him now.

As for my children, how can I help them overcome their lack of trust? Some of their desire to have their own way is simply a fight against the flesh, the same as mine. But if I model myself after Jesus, hopefully their disobedience will lessen, and their desire to follow Jesus will take over.

If you want to get a great picture of who Jesus is, just look through Matthew 14. At the beginning of the chapter, Jesus has just learned of the death of John the Baptist. He withdraws to be alone and is followed by crowds of people. In one of the worst scenarios, the death of a friend, Jesus shows His true character.

He's compassionate (verses 13-14) and kind (verse 16). He provides (verse 19), and he is prayerful (verse 23) and encouraging (verse 27).

Having a true picture of the character of God and His Son, Jesus, is essential to defeating the control freak within. When I know who He is, I know I can trust

Him. When I know I can trust Him, I know I can stop trying to run the show.

Now that we are on boy number 3, I have learned that there are some things I can control, and some that I cannot. There are things I thought I wanted to control, but really, what is the point? As I have become more comfortable in this parenting gig, I have seen that every scenario is not going to play out to the worst case. If he wears mismatching clothes to church, is there truly anything bad in that?

Some trust in chariots and some in horses, but we trust in the name of the Lord our God. ~Psalm 20:7

I'll try to turn off the control freak inside and tell her to chill out. Now, if I could only get those boys to find their shoes ...

CHAPTER 6

Anger Awakened

My dear brothers and sisters, take note of this: Everyone should be quick to listen, slow to speak and slow to become angry, because human anger does not produce the righteousness that God desires. ~James 1:19-20

I think it is safe to say that I have always had a temper—at least, as long as I can remember. In my youth, it mainly surfaced while playing basketball or tennis, and a good portion of the time, the anger was directed at myself. If I wasn't performing well or was making silly mistakes, I might let my frustration take over and shut me down.

In relationships, I never have been one to yell or argue too much. I'm not saying there aren't differences in opinion, but I generally haven't become angry and yelled at someone.

Then I had kids.

I don't know what it is about having children that turned this switch on, but I wish I could turn it back off. When Zachary was born and was so little and sweet and tiny, I never pictured myself yelling at him in anger. It's hard to imagine when they are newborns that they could anger you to the point of a meltdown. Fast-forward six years, and one word from one of them can set me off like an atomic bomb.

I'm going to get real here. We've all got dirty laundry (and not just the literal kind), and some of mine happens to fall in the category of self-control. I have been known to throw a toy or two (not at them, but in general). Maybe I've stepped on something they were supposed to pick up, and I throw it into their closet. Maybe it's a toy that annoys me for some reason, and they aren't listening and putting it away like they were told. Regardless, there is no excuse. This is not acceptable behavior. Why do I say that? Because when they do it, they get in trouble for not controlling their anger.

Whoops.

So what is it that makes me so angry? Why do I let things get me to my boiling point? In a great book called *Triggers* by Amber Mills Lia and Wendy Speake, the authors talk about all the things that can bring you to that point. (I recommend it for every parent out there, especially if you struggle with anger.) For me, some of my triggers, or hot buttons, are things like:

- Being tired
- Having a plan in my head that my kids aren't following

- Repeated disobedience
- Kids bickering with each other
- Messy toys

Any one of these things, or a combination of them, can set me off. I might even start calm, but after the hundredth time of telling them to stop, I lose my cool. I can go from 0 to 100 in 2.5 seconds, and often, I'm not dealing with the true issues; instead I'm letting things fester or ignoring a problem. (For instance, why am I telling them 100 times without any consequence?)

As a result, I can end up hurting the little people that I love. I say things too harshly, or I tear them down. I belittle them or berate them. Not only does this tear apart the little hearts that I should protect, but it also teaches them the wrong way to handle anger. What will they do when they get angry? More than likely they will repeat or reenact what they have seen. How can I teach them the right way when I don't even do it myself?

When I look at Jesus and His life here on Earth, He gives plenty of examples of how I should handle anger. One thing I think I should understand, though, is the difference between a righteous anger and a sinful anger.

Jesus shows us in John 2:13-22 what would be considered a righteous anger. He goes to the temple where people should be humble and worshipping God, and they are treating it like a "den of thieves." They took a sacred, holy place and turned it into a greedy marketplace. What did Jesus do? He told them to get out and overturned the tables!

I've taught this lesson with my children and in Sunday School, and this one is always tricky. My kids saw this as Jesus sinning because he became angry and overturned the tables. We have been careful to discuss and differentiate here because they (and we) should understand the difference between righteous and sinful anger.

Righteous anger is showing deep displeasure over sin. Things like abuse, racism, and child sex-trafficking should upset me and make me sick.

Examples of this in the Bible are Nehemiah in Nehemiah 5:6 or David in Psalm 139:19-22. Both Nehemiah and David have anger toward the actions of ungodly people.

Sinful anger would be reacting quickly and seeking the vengeance myself instead of leaving it in God's hands.

I think the key difference is, does my anger honor God?

Psalm 4:4 says, "In your anger, do not sin; when you are on your beds, search your hearts and be silent."

(By the way, this is a great memory verse for parents and children alike!)

When we are angry with our children, are we angry at sin, or are we just irritated with whatever they are doing and want to get it off our chest?

My dear brothers and sisters, take note of this: Everyone should be quick to listen, slow to speak and slow to become angry, because human anger does not produce the righteousness that God desires. ~James 1:19-20

I think this verse should be framed in my house somewhere.

When my little people push my buttons, or make me want to explode, I need to slow down. Even if they are disobeying, that is not an excuse for me to tear them apart. Should I discipline? YES. Should they know what they did wrong? DEFINITELY. The key is keeping myself under the control of the Holy Spirit and not letting my flesh take over.

And when it does take over ...

I ask for their forgiveness. I explain to them that I should have controlled my temper. I should not have thrown their toy. Should they have obeyed? Yes. Is there still a consequence for their disobedience? Yes. But I try to always acknowledge when I know I have crossed the line and flown off the handle. They always forgive. Even in my sin, God can use those moments and still teach them—and teach me. He can use all of that, if we let Him. Every moment, every mess-up, every victory, we offer to Him and say, "It's yours."

In my moments of weakness, my children can see me as the imperfect human I am and learn to follow Jesus, despite that.

CHAPTER 7

But What about My Pillowcase?

*Trust in the Lord with all your heart
and lean not on your own understanding;
in all your ways submit to him,
and he will make your paths straight.* ~Psalm 3:5-6

It was a cold night, and I was getting the big boys ready for bed. Their room is upstairs, and when it is freezing or below outside, their room can get pretty chilly. We have a little space heater we use for these occasions, and I explained when we purchased it that they are not to bother it. Even though it has a safety feature that will turn it off if it gets knocked over, they have been told not to touch it or put anything near it.

Can you tell where this is going?

I had just turned the heater on and began helping one of them. I then turned my back. By the time I turned back around, I saw Zachary's pillow lying across the front of the heater. I panicked.

"Zachary! Your pillow!"

I immediately grabbed the pillow, pulled it away from the heater, and quickly unplugged the heater. I could see that it had already melted the pillowcase (it must have been nylon), so I pulled that off. The pillow protector underneath had a big brownish-black circle where it had been burned. The heater had the remnants of melted nylon stuck to it.

"Zachary! You burned the pillow! Don't you remember me telling you not to put anything on the heater? Wow, I am so glad I was up here when this happened. The whole house could have burned down! What happened? Did it get knocked off the bed?"

"No."

"Did you put it on there?"

"Yes."

"You put it on there on purpose? Why?"

"I don't know."

"You don't know? Look at this pillowcase! It's melted! It's burned!"

"I thought it was just air. I thought it was a good idea."

"You thought it would be good?"

"I wanted to see what would happen."

"It could have burned everything—that's what could have happened."

At this point, he was crying. I wasn't yelling; I was more in panic mode, trying to make sure this never happened again. I felt like he was scared and upset, so I lightened up a little.

"Zachary, I'm just glad we caught it before something really bad happened. Are you okay?"

"Mmmhmm."

"Okay, let me get this stuff out of here."

"My striped pillowcase! Don't throw it away!"

"Zachary, it's ruined. There's a hole in the middle of it. It can't be used anymore."

"No! I want to keep it!"

"So, the house could have caught fire, but you're upset about the pillowcase?"

"Yes! I love it! I don't want you to get rid of it!"

I am still cringing as I relive this. Just the thought of what could have happened makes me sick to my stomach. They have so many blankets and stuffed animals, and any one of those things could have ended up on that heater at any given time. It could have been in the middle of the night, when one of them did something in their sleep. (I tend to go worst-case scenario fairly often.)

Judging by the look on his face, I thought that it had scared him and that he felt awful about what had happened. He probably did. But what shocked me was the fact that instead of being upset that he could have started a fire, burned the house down, and lost everything he owns, he was upset that his white pillowcase with blue stripes was not recoverable.
Focused on the immediate loss, on what he could see, he got hysterical and cried when I tried to get rid of it. I don't know why he had such an attachment to that pillowcase. It wasn't even a special one with characters or some sentimental value. Zachary simply has a hard time letting things go, which makes me wonder ...

What am I hanging on to that has no value? What am I attached to that I think I love? What is my pillowcase?

What is distracting me from the fact that I have been saved? My salvation is secure. I have accepted Jesus as my Savior, and I have been spared from the fire, from an eternity without Him. But what earthly thing am I hanging on to instead of finding joy?

I have found myself still clinging to things I think are important. Sin can still have a shiny allure. Just because I have been redeemed does not mean I no longer find the ways of the world appealing. The more time I spend chasing after the Lord, and in His Word, the less desirable the world will seem.

The lie that has tripped me up in the past is that "giving things up" will be a huge loss. I don't know why I think that, but all I can see is what is right in front of me, and what I think I am losing. I'm clutching my pillowcase, afraid to let go.

> *I can anticipate the response that is coming: "I know that all God's commands are spiritual, but I'm not. Isn't this also your experience?" Yes. I'm full of myself—after all, I've spent a long time in sin's prison. What I don't understand about myself is that I decide one way, but then I act another, doing things I absolutely despise. So if I can't be trusted to figure out what is best for myself and then do it, it becomes obvious that God's command is necessary.*
>
> *But I need something more! For if I know the law but still can't keep it, and if the power of sin within me keeps sabotaging my best intentions, I obviously need help! I realize that I don't have what it takes. I can will it, but I can't do it. I decide to do good, but I don't really do it; I decide not to do bad, but then I do it anyway. My decisions, such as they are, don't result in actions. Something has gone wrong deep within me and gets the better of me every time.*
>
> *It happens so regularly that it's predictable. The moment I decide to do good, sin is there to trip me up. I truly delight in God's commands, but*

it's pretty obvious that not all of me joins in that delight. Parts of me covertly rebel, and just when I least expect it, they take charge.

I've tried everything and nothing helps. I'm at the end of my rope. Is there no one who can do anything for me? Isn't that the real question?

The answer, thank God, is that Jesus Christ can and does. He acted to set things right in this life of contradictions where I want to serve God with all my heart and mind, but am pulled by the influence of sin to do something totally different. ~Romans 7:14-25, The Message

Even Paul, the one God used to write quite a few books in the New Testament, had the same struggles as we do. For me, it helps to see things from a different angle. When I look at something my child has done and think it is foolish, or unthinkable, God tends to hand me a flashlight, show me my own sin, and say, "Here, how does this seem to you now?"

I pray that I can stop battling for the things I think I want and open my eyes to what Jesus has already done for me. I pray that I can let go, drop the pillowcase, and turn to God and praise Him for His mercy. Friends, I pray that we will stop hanging on to what we think we've lost and realize what we have been saved from. Within that knowledge, we can then step out of the sin, and live in the joy that Christ has given us.

CHAPTER 8

Inadequate

My grace is sufficient for you, for my power is made perfect in weakness. ~2 Corinthians 12:9

Some days, I just feel like a complete failure. Okay, so sometimes it stretches into more than a day. As I write this, I am in one of those stretches now. I feel like I am scraping, clawing, fighting my way out of a hole, and I cannot get myself out. Every day, I am pulling myself up, and then someone throws a barrel full of water at me and knocks me down. I feel like I am never caught up, never ahead.

Ever since my youngest, Lincoln, was born, I have gotten out of the habit of cooking supper. I grew tired of the same meals, tired of looking for new ones, and tired of putting the effort into making them. I worry about not cooking, about no one eating healthy, and about exactly how many peanut-butter-and-jelly sandwiches it will take to turn them into one. I feel too stressed to think up a meal, stressed that I didn't think up a meal, and stressed that there is no end in sight to this vicious cycle.

I'm busy at work. I'm tired of feeling like I don't know the answers. I have an endless task list with not enough of them marked complete.

I want to make the time to spend with the Lord, time to write, and time to spend with my husband. We've been meaning to have "date night" for going on three months now.

Am I spending enough time with the kids? Shouldn't I read to them more? How do we decide which sports they should do? Is the homework finished? How soon until the next birthday? When can we take them on vacation?

My brain is in overdrive and doesn't want to shut off. I have not been sleeping well—or enough. As a result, I get crabby, impatient, crazy, and even mean.

It never ends. There are days that I just want to give up. Yesterday, back to back, I managed to bump Lincoln's chin into my shoulder and then straight up just poke him in the eye. He bawled. So did I.

It's times like these when I look around and think, "How am I supposed to do all this?"
For we do not have a high priest who is unable to empathize with our weaknesses, but we have one who has been tempted in every way, just as we are—yet he did not sin. ~Hebrews 4:15

Be strong and courageous. Do not be afraid or terrified because of them, for the Lord your God goes with you; he will never leave you nor forsake you. ~Deuteronomy 31:6

The Lord himself goes before you and will be with you; he will never leave you nor forsake you. Do not be afraid; do not be discouraged. ~Deuteronomy 31:8

When all is out of control, when everything falls apart, when circumstances are constantly changing ... I can go to His Word. The never-changing, the absolute truth, the living, breathing Word of God. If you look back through this chapter, what do you see? *I feel ... I'm worried ... I'm tired ... I don't know.* I am not the perfect parent. Some days, I'd say I'm downright awful.

I love my kids with all my heart; that doesn't change. Sometimes though, my attitude stinks. I believe I have found the common thread to why these situations start to overwhelm me: I'm trying to do it all. I'm trying to do it on my own.

I know you have all been there. I'm betting that some of you are there right now, with me.

So stop.

Just stop.

Stop trying to fix everything.

Stop trying to BE everything.

Yes, you will fail. But do you know what the beautiful news is? You don't have to do it on your own. God wants us to run to Him. He wants us to throw our hands up to Him and give Him control. Jesus knows how hard life is. He lived it, here on earth. He knows what it is to have human emotions, to be exhausted, to be beaten down. He wants to carry our burdens.

Come to me, all you who are weary and burdened, and I will give you rest. Take my yoke upon you and learn from me, for I am gentle and humble in heart, and you will find rest for your souls. For my yoke is easy and my burden is light. ~Matthew 11:28-30

Instead of carrying the weight, instead of scrambling to get out of the pit on your own, instead of worrying ...

Go to Him. Rest in His Word. Stand on His Promises.

It's okay that we are inadequate. We will never measure up on our own. God does not leave us in our feeble state.

But God demonstrates his own love for us in this: While we were still sinners, Christ died for us. ~Romans 5:8

You don't have to wait until you have things together to run to God. Take your mess, your tiredness, your crummy attitude—all your darkness—and lay it bare before Him. Kneel as a beggar before Him. He will have you rise, for he does not see you this way. He will clothe you in Christ's perfection and count you as His heir. Rejoice friends. We are all inadequate.

CHAPTER 9

It's Not about Me

"Come, follow me, and I will make you fishers of people." At once they left their nets and followed Him.
~Matthew 4:19-20

Even before my children were born, before I was pregnant with them, I loved them. I know that sounds strange, but I just knew my heart; I knew that I wanted to become a mother.

Although I had a picture of parenthood and how I would feel, I don't think you can ever be fully prepared. I knew there would be times of great joy, and times of great difficulty. What I didn't realize (and honestly, until you are deep in it, I don't know that you can) is the level of commitment it takes to be a good parent.

For one, as a mother, my body is sacrificed, at least for a time. I don't mean that I can't get my pre-baby body back (although that is a struggle for me). Essentially though, I am giving my body up for a time to carry and grow my baby. Some moms have more issues than others during pregnancy. I wouldn't say I had difficult pregnancies, but they were ... uncomfortable.

Bringing my miracle(s) into the world ... well, we all know that is no picnic. I am definitely putting that little life ahead of my own to bring him into the world. Breastfeeding? Again, I am putting the baby's needs above my own and literally pouring myself into his life. From toddler to teenager, I am always their comfort. A mama's arms are the refuge for tear-soaked cheeks, scraped knees, and broken hearts.

Moms talk about needing "me time." Having little ones, I am lucky to count a shower as my "me time." It is vital to my sanity to take care of myself, to take breaks when I need them, and to keep myself healthy. I think the part I didn't really think about before becoming a parent is there is no true "break." I never stop being responsible for these little lives, even if I do get to take breathers. I frequently think, *Why do they always have to be fed?!* I can't just stop feeding them because I am tired—their lives depend on me.

Daily, I am filling up little hearts and investing in them, teaching them, and pouring love into them. It is a constant demand.

It is not my intention to sound negative, quite the opposite. All these ways that I am stretched, and pushed, and tested, they grow me in my faith.

When I choose to follow Jesus, I lay it all down. I listen to His call and lay my own life down; I die to self. Look at the life of Jesus. His ministry was a constant pouring out on the people. He was teaching, comforting, feeding. People followed Him everywhere. The demands on Jesus were unreal, yet He never complained and never pushed anyone aside. He always put others first, always gave of Himself.

It's so hard to imagine that Jesus was able to do all of this without ever complaining, not even once. Every time He was needed, every time He had to put Himself last, He did it with perfection.

With each passing day as a parent, I find that I need to lay my selfish desires aside. When I have the baby in one arm and am fixing PB & J with the other, while getting ready for work, I stay focused, but the focus is not on me. My eyes should be on Jesus and how He wants to use me.

If He hadn't given me the gift of being a parent, maybe I would have missed the things I am learning about Him. I am not saying that everyone should be a parent—not at all. But for me, I need to see it lived and to experience these lessons right in front of my face.

Being a parent is teaching me how to follow Jesus. In the down-and-dirty trenches, day after day, this is what it looks like to die to self.

> *Those who live according to the flesh have their minds set on what the flesh desires; but those who live in accordance with the Spirit have their minds set on what the Spirit desires. The mind governed by the flesh is death, but the mind governed by the Spirit is life and peace. The mind governed by the flesh is hostile to*

God; it does not submit to God's law, nor can it do so. Those who are in the realm of the flesh cannot please God.

You, however, are not in the realm of the flesh but are in the realm of the Spirit, if indeed the Spirit of God lives in you. And if anyone does not have the Spirit of Christ, they do not belong to Christ. But if Christ is in you, then even though your body is subject to death because of sin, the Spirit gives life. Or you, your body is dead because of sin, yet your spirit is alive because of righteousness. And if the Spirit of him who raised Jesus from the dead is living in you, he who raised Christ from the dead will also give life to your mortal bodies because of his Spirit who lives in you. ~Romans 8:5-11

I am not perfect. I frequently let my flesh have control and lose my temper or get crabby. I want to be selfish because I am tired. I don't want one more thing asked of me for the day, but that is not what Jesus called me to. He called me to drop my net and to follow Him, to drop what I think I have to have, let go of what I think I deserve or need, and simply follow. These little lives need me. They need to see Jesus in me. Jesus never promised an easy life, but He did promise to send us help.

And I will ask the Father, and he will give you another advocate to help you and be with you forever— the Spirit of truth. The world cannot accept him, because it neither sees him nor knows him. But you know him, for he lives with you and will be in you. I will not leave you as orphans; I will come to you. ~John 14:16-18

If you are feeling spent, at the end of your rope, or like you just don't have one more drop of energy left in you, you are not alone. Yes, Jesus called us to a life of serving others, of pouring out of ourselves. But He gave us the perfect example in His life here on earth. When you feel like the flesh is taking over, call to Jesus.

Remember His sacrifice and His promises. Know that in these battles of parenthood, He is refining you. And in the process, your children will know what it looks like to follow Jesus.

CHAPTER 10

Peel Away

This third I will put into the fire; I will refine them like silver and test them like gold. They will call on my name and I will answer them; I will say, "They are my people," and they will say, "The Lord is our God."
~Zechariah 13:9

I am at my worst when I am tired, which is probably a true statement for most people. What is one of the most popular things to ask a new parent?

"Is the baby sleeping?"
"Are you getting any sleep?"

I must say (and some people may hate me for this) that all our boys have been great sleepers. We're talking at six to eight weeks old they were sleeping six to seven hours each night, and improving with time. When I tell people that, they tell me how lucky we are.

I know. I know how amazing that is, and my expanded answer has become, "God knows how crabby I am if I don't get sleep and is therefore protecting my children by making them good sleepers." I give Him the glory because I know what a bear I can be if I am running too ragged.

But even if they are great sleepers, life still hurries along. I am still busy working, caring for them, cleaning—whatever the tasks may be. When that happens (and this happens to ALL of us), things get pushed to the side. My time with the Lord gets pushed aside. A layer grows. I am rushing, pushing, hurrying them to bed and getting annoyed when they delay. A layer grows. I get distracted, and I lose focus. A layer grows. I'm greedy for my time, forgetting that they are little people who need me. I just feel like the victim of their disobedience. Self. Foolishness. Pride. Layer, layer, layer.

As a kid, I loved to read, and because my mom worked in a library, I had no shortage of books at my disposal. One of my all-time favorites (I have many) is *The Chronicles of Narnia,* the timeless collection by C.S. Lewis. I loved being swept away into this other world. The stories gripped my heart ... and still do. I have reread them as an adult, multiple times. It's funny how God can pull pictures or words from your memory at the right time to help you hear what He is saying.

In this instance, I remembered Eustace. In *The Voyage of the Dawn Treador,* Eustace is a nasty, selfish, whiney boy who gets unwillingly sent to Narnia. He is a burden and thorn in everyone's side. They eventually get to an island where he wanders off by himself. He comes across a dragon, who seems sick or old, and Eustace happens to see it die, noticing then the treasure that the dragon was guarding. In his foolishness, greed, and selfishness, he takes some of the treasure and then ends up falling asleep amongst the gold.

When he wakes up, he thinks he is surrounded by dragons on each side, but it is he who has become a dragon. He tries to scratch away at the dragon skin. He peels scale after scale, layer after layer. No difference. He can't peel away the layers of ugliness he has built upon himself. It is here where he meets Aslan, the Lion. He is scared, but he knows the only way to get the dragon skin off is to let the Lion tear it away. The Lion pierces deep and peels back all the layers. He tears it all off, pulls it all away, until the dragon is gone. Eustace bathes in the waters and becomes a boy again.

I know the Holy Spirit brought this story to my mind for a reason. I needed to see myself as Eustace. I needed to see all the layers I had placed upon myself—the selfishness, the foolishness, the pride. Why am I seeing myself as a victim of my kids' disobedience?

"Why are they DOING this to me?"

What if Jesus said that to me? Does Jesus talk down to us and shame us when we disobey? No. It's always love. It's always truth, but it's also always love.

I think about the woman at the well, in John chapter 4. Jesus could have shamed her. He didn't have to even speak to her or be around her. Instead, He gave her hope. He acknowledged her sin, but focused on what He could give her.

I need God to tear deep, to tear through all these layers I've built up around myself. I need to allow the great King, the Lion, to pierce through the sin and tear away all that is not of Him. It hurts. Oh yes, it hurts. But it's good.

I can feel the layers falling to the ground, and I step into the soothing waters of who He is. I want to bathe in His goodness and heal in His waters.

Once it is all torn away—the self, the foolishness, the pride—then He can show us who He means us to be. It is no longer a "task" to follow Him, but a deep desire. I pray that I can catch myself before I let any new layers form. No matter what is going on in my life, I want to stay true to who He wants me to be, and follow Him closely. Not because I feel obligated, but because where else would I want to turn? There is no one like Jesus, which makes me think of Peter in John 6:68 ...

Lord, to whom shall we go? You have the words of eternal life.

When parenting has drained you, when your job has defeated you, when people forsake you ... turn to Jesus. He can peel away the layers and make you whole again.

Oh ... and if a rare opportunity to take a nap appears before you, TAKE IT.

CHAPTER 11

A Boy's Broken Heart

*Search me, God, and know my heart;
test me and know my anxious thoughts.
See if there is any offensive way in me,
and lead me in the way everlasting.* ~Psalm 139:23-24

It's torture to watch your child in pain, and I know many, many people have to see their children go through horrific things. We have not had to endure even a drop in the bucket compared to some, but seeing your child in any amount of pain is too much. Of my three boys so far, it seems as if Gavin has had the most ... incidents.

When Gavin was born, he had to stay in the Neonatal Intensive Care Unit (NICU) for ten days. He had group B strep and had to undergo plenty of needles and tests. Although compared to the other babies there he was pretty healthy, it was still hard not to be able to take our baby home right away.

As an infant, Gavin had ear infections that resulted in a burst eardrum three times. He also had many bouts with croup, one of which sent him to the emergency room. His other ER trip came when we were at a store looking at cell phones, and he pulled a cord that snapped back and popped him in his eye.

He fell at church and slammed his cheek into the side of a pew. That one left a pretty mark. He happened to be coming down with a stomach bug at the same time and ended up throwing up all over my husband Stefan that day.

For me, the worst of any of these was last summer when he shut his finger in the car door. (I spoke briefly about this in an earlier chapter). I was pregnant with Lincoln, and the boys and I stopped at a store on the way home from church. As we were getting out of the vehicle, I was making sure they didn't run out in the parking lot.

Gavin got out first, so I told him to stand with his hand on the side of the vehicle, to ensure he didn't go anywhere. After Zachary got out, I shut the door. What I didn't notice was that Gavin had slid his fingers to the opening of the door at the last second.

I could not stop the door from shutting, and I could not tell him to move. I was frozen, mute, helpless. The door slammed, with Gavin's finger inside. I had to open the door to get his finger out. (I would gladly endure all three childbirths again before I would relive that moment.)

There we were, standing in the parking lot—a pregnant mama; Gavin screaming, bleeding, and crying; and Zachary freaking out because he saw blood. I stood there, not knowing what to do, until I remembered there were paper towels on the floor of the car somewhere. Fortunately, we were close to our house, so we just got back in and I sped home. I cried with Gavin the whole way. It was a rough couple hours, but he toughed it out. He ended up losing that nail, but there was no lasting damage.

Despite his many injuries, Gavin is a pretty happy kid. When he does something, he does it with gusto—that goes for doing something happily, or choosing to disobey. When he disobeys, it is in grand form.

Lately, he has been having a rough time. I don't know if it is his age or the fact that we have been phasing out naps, but recently, he has been very difficult. (Perhaps it is because we made him a middle child.) It really is out of character for him to be consistently disobedient and disrespectful for a prolonged amount of time. Usually it comes in spurts. I finally decided to ask him about it.

"Gavin, is something wrong?"

"I'm sad."

"Why are you sad?"

"I don't know. I am just sad all the time."

He couldn't give me a reason. Gavin tends to operate in the extremes and can turn at the drop of a hat, but I saw that something was going on with him. When he gets corrected, he has been doing things like saying, "I'm stupid. Everyone hates me," and even hitting or scratching himself. I think some of this is a phase, and some of it may be middle-child syndrome. No matter what the cause, it is always difficult to watch your child go through pain. In all of these things, at the heart of it, I can see his brokenness.

I remember Zachary going through a time when he said his heart was broken. It may have been around the same age, or even a little younger. I believe this is the beginning of them feeling their own sin. It is deeply saddening as a parent to see your child intentionally sinning for those first times. Maybe it is their first lie or outright disobedience, but seeing them lose that innocence (and realizing you can't save them) leaves you feeling powerless.

Although it is agonizing to watch, my kids need to recognize their own sin and realize their need for a Savior. They need to see that they need Jesus. I want to protect them from everything. I want to spare them from pain. But without the pain or the realization of their need for a Savior, I rob them of the One who can heal them.

I cannot make my children's decisions. It is ultimately their choice to make, to follow Jesus or not. Even though I cannot act for them, as their parent, I can do three very crucial things for them.

I cover them in prayer, and I can always improve on this one. The best way to protect and be proactive for my kids is to pray on their behalf. They need intentional, specific prayers over their lives. Behind many great Christians is a praying mom, dad, or grandparent. Our prayers matter.

I cover them in love. That sounds basic, but it is always harder in the moment, especially moments like these:

Love is patient, love is kind. It does not envy, it does not boast, it is not proud. It does not dishonor others, it is not self-seeking, it is not easily angered, it keeps no record of wrongs. Love does not delight in evil but rejoices with the truth. It always protects, always trusts, always hopes, always perseveres. Love never fails. ~1 Corinthians 13:4-8a

Lastly, and what I think is the toughest, I must live it. My life must lead them to Jesus. Who is a more accurate witness to my daily behavior than my own kids? They hear my words, but most of all they see my actions. They need to see me leaning on Jesus, to see that He is the only way to fix their broken heart. I want to show them that they can take everything to Him—not just big things, but the little things too. The most loving thing I can do for someone is show them the way to Jesus.

I know Gavin has an understanding for his age that he wants to follow Jesus. He can be very insightful for a four-year-old, wise beyond his years. I know as he goes through this rough patch, he is testing and learning his boundaries. He is searching and finding his faith.

Lord, let me be a gentle breeze to help guide him in the right direction. When he falls, let me be there to show him You are there. As much as it hurts a mama to say it, I cannot fix my boy's broken heart, but I can lead him to the One who can.

CHAPTER 12

Desire to Be Close

As the deer pants for streams of water, so my soul pants for you, my God. My soul thirsts for God, for the living God. ~Psalm 42:1-2a

I love to cuddle with my boys. I can't help but grab them, pull them close, and get my hugs in whenever I can. There is just something about being physically near them that breathes life into me. Whether we're watching a movie or reading books, I snatch up every moment I can to get them on my lap because I know that they won't fit there forever.

Lincoln is my baby. He's still little enough to need constant holding, cuddling, and carrying. I know that once he learns to walk, that will lessen. Right now, he is sick with a nasty cold that has run its course through our whole household.

Unfortunately, it seems to be sticking with him longer than I'd like. He's got the snotty nose, goopy eyes—all the yuckiness. He needed a nap, but I didn't want him to cry and get extra snotty, so rather than just lay him down right away, I held him close for a while, on my shoulder, drawing him near. I felt this strong bond with him at that moment. He felt like an extension of my heart, as if he was still part of me, like when I carried him in my belly and I could feel my heartstrings connected straight to him. It made me wonder, is this how God feels about us, His creation? Is God longing to hold us close? Is that how He sees us when we come to Him and pray?

Every day when I get home from work and Zachary is home from school, I tend to ask him the same thing. "How was your day?" He hates it.

He finally got angry one day and said, "I hate it when people ask me that!"

I can sympathize with him. He has just gone through a full day at school, being questioned, being around people. For him, that is exhausting. The last thing he wants when he gets home is to be drilled about his day. I don't ask him to annoy him. I don't need to know every aspect of his day. I know what his schedule is. In fact, I can check the school calendar to see the activities he did and the lunch he had. I can look through his bookbag and see the papers he's brought home.

But that is not the point, is it? I just want to hear him talk to me. I want to hear how he felt the day went. I want to see his excitement, or his disappointment, in the day's events. I want him to share his heart with me because I love him. When I am not with him, or Gavin, or Lincoln, I miss them.

Isn't that what God wants from us in prayer? To hear about our day from our perspective?

Gavin, my middle son, is such a "feeler." He is very passionate and expressive. I never have to wonder what or how he is feeling because you can either see it in his face, or he's telling you about it with his large vocabulary. Sometimes he just follows me around. At times that has irritated me because usually I am in the middle of some task, and I end up stepping on him.

"Gavin, what are you doing?"

He looks at me with his big eyes and says, "Mom, I just want to be close to you, and be where you are, because I love you."

Oh Gavin, he always gets me right in the heart.

What if I followed God with that attitude? Lord, I just want to be close to You, and be where You are, because I love You.

I want to help them with requests. If they need something, I want to know so that I can help them. I may already know they need help, but sometimes I need them to realize they need help so that they can learn from it.

I want to make things better for them. I want to help them solve problems. If they have overcome a problem or had a success? I want to hear that too. Even if it is about catching a new Pokemon, I want them to share it with me—not that I particularly need to know about Pokemon, but I want to hear their heart and what they care about.

I think of all these ways I desire to communicate with them and think ... isn't that what God wants? For us to come to him with everything?

Tired?

My soul finds rest in God alone; my salvation comes from Him. He alone is my rock and my salvation; He is my fortress, I will never be shaken. ~Psalm 62:1-2

Sick?

Lord my God, I called to You for help, and You healed me. ~Psalm 30:2

Scared?

So do not fear, for I am with you;
do not be dismayed, for I am your God.
I will strengthen you and help you;
I will uphold you with my righteous right hand.
~Isaiah 41:10

As their mother, it is my natural desire to comfort them, to nurture them. How much more does God want to do these things for us, through prayer?

When I talk to God, He already knows everything, right? He knows every event that has happened, or will happen. So why do I need to pray? Am I going to change God's mind when I pray?

When Zachary was four, I signed him up for T-ball. Since we are big baseball fans (GO CARDINALS!), this was an exciting moment for me. I told Zachary I had signed him up to play, and he lost his mind. He was so upset and refused to play. I tried talking to him on several occasions, telling him it wouldn't be scary, that it would be fun, and he would love it if he would just try. He would not play. I decided it was best just to cancel it and try again next year, rather than traumatize him over the experience.

The next summer rolled around, and I tried again. This time, Gavin was four, and Zachary was five, so they could play together on the same team. Gavin was thrilled. He couldn't wait to get out there to play. Zachary was still hesitant, but he agreed to try it this time.

On the way to their first game, we were in the car, and Zachary said, "It's going to take a long time to get there."

I said, "Zachary, you've never been to the field we're going to. It isn't that far."

"Yes, it is! It takes a long time to get to the Cardinals!"

Stefan and I looked at each other.

"Zachary, you aren't playing at Busch Stadium ..."

"Uh huh, we're playing with the Cardinals!"

It all made sense.

"Is that why you were so scared to play, because you thought you were playing for the St. Louis Cardinals?"

"Yes!"

Perspective.

No wonder the poor boy was terrified. He thought he was going to play professional baseball with grown men. Once we finally realized that and saw his true fears and expectations, we were able to reassure him that he would not be facing an impossible situation. He would be learning T-ball with other kids his age.

It's funny how a little communication can change a situation.

How many times have I built things up in my head to more than what they really are? How much grief, fear, and heartache have I put on myself when I didn't have to?

God does not want me to try to bear these things on my own. He wants me to come to Him. He longs to be close to me. He desires to know my heart. He wants to comfort me. All these things that I want for and from my children, God wants for me.

This is the confidence we have in approaching God: that if we ask anything according to his will, he hears us. And if we know that he hears us—whatever we ask—we know that we have what we asked of him. ~1John 5:14

When I look at prayer from this angle, I think it really makes a difference. I shouldn't look at prayer as an obligation. It isn't a daily duty to check off the list. It is an experience.

My sheep listen to my voice; I know them, and they follow me. I give them eternal life, and they shall never perish; no one will snatch them out of my hand. My Father, who has given them to me, is greater than all; no one can snatch them out of my Father's hand. I and the Father are one. ~John 10:27-30

Growing closer to the Maker of the universe is a privilege. I should just want to follow Him around to be close to Him, because I love Him.

CHAPTER 13

Milk for the Soul

For the word of God is alive and active. Sharper than any double-edged sword, it penetrates even to dividing soul and spirit, joints and marrow; it judges the thoughts and attitudes of the heart. ~Hebrews 4:12

I have been fortunate in that I have been able to breastfeed all three of my boys. With Zachary, I was able to do so for about nine or ten months. Then I became pregnant with Gavin, and my body could focus only on growing the new person and not feeding my firstborn.

I was able to feed Gavin longer, I think because of our new living arrangement. After Gavin was born, Stefan's mother, Marcia (or Gran), came to live with us and watch our boys while we worked. Because of this (amazing) situation, I was able to nurse more and pump less; therefore, I nursed Gavin until he was over a year old.

Now I have Lincoln, who is currently eight months old. In all this time, I have learned so much about nursing, and I am continually amazed at God's design.

I do want to be clear that I understand not everyone is able to breastfeed. There are plenty of circumstances when it is just not possible, and there should not be any judgement or guilt because of this. Every situation is unique.

Before having kids, I didn't really know very much about a mother's milk, and with each of my children, I think I have learned more about it. There are several things that really blow my mind when it comes to breastmilk.

For the first four to six months of a baby's life, all they need is their mama's milk. When you think about that, and all the growing, changing, and developing that they do in these stages, it is truly amazing. Every nutrient, every protection, is right there, ready-made for them.

As the baby grows and his needs change, the milk changes too. If you have ever seen the first milk produced and compared it to milk from a few months down the road, there is a difference. It really is magical, how it morphs and changes into exactly what the baby needs. The same thing occurs when a baby is sick. A picture was floating around the Internet a while back, showing the difference—within a couple days—showing the way a mom's milk changed. When a baby nurses and is sick, the milk can cater to what the baby needs.
Another fascinating thing is mom's supply vs. baby's demand. Cluster feedings, or additional feedings, are ways that baby can help mom bolster her supply. Also, it doesn't take very long for mom to replenish her supply after being emptied.

Surprisingly, I found out there are other uses for it too. (Before trying any of these I recommend you do your own research or ask your doctor.) This may sound strange, but because of the antibodies in it, some moms say that their breastmilk can help heal too. Ear infection? A couple drops to the ear. Eye irritation? A couple drops to the eye. Using it as a facial cleanser or an antiseptic for cuts/scrapes are just a couple more uses I have read about. Really, this stuff is magnificent!

The bottom line is that babies need their mama's milk. They long for it, enjoy it, and are comforted by it. It is essential to their growth, development, and survival. Breastmilk is powerful, versatile, and full of life.

Since I am in this stage of life—the stage of nursing, and pumping, and centering schedules around feedings—it is no wonder that thinking about the versatility and importance of breastmilk made me think of God's Word. As a follower of Jesus, the Bible is essential to my life. Sometimes you hear breastmilk referred to as "liquid gold," and as a believer, God's Word is definitely a great treasure.

God's Word is alive. That means it speaks to us every time we read it, sometimes in new ways. Many, many times, in rereading a passage, I pull something different out of it than I have before. It is what we need, when we need it. The message grows with us and finds new depths as we mature.

Like babies depend on mama's milk for survival, so I should depend on my Father's Word. I should long for it, enjoy it, and be comforted by it. Is a baby with a bottle or at his mother's breast completing a chore? No, he is filling up, getting fueled. He is being soothed and healed.

God's Word is powerful and rich. It's nourishment to get me through the day. It's a defense against the enemy, and protection against the worst of times. It's cleansing and refreshing. God's Word is crucial to my well-being, my purpose, my joy.

Your word is a lamp for my feet, a light on my path. ~Psalm 119:105

Like newborn babies, crave pure spiritual milk, so that by it you may grow up in your salvation. ~1 Peter 2:2

It is imperative that I view God's Word from the proper perspective. It isn't just something that is nice to have, or that I hear at church or on Christmas. His Word is alive, indispensable, and vital to my everyday life.

I am the biggest failure when it comes to this—I admit it—so understand that I am talking to myself here more than anyone. Dive in daily, even if for a moment at first, and nourish yourself. What a difference it makes when I don't spiritually starve myself. Fill up on the sweet, perfect Word of God!

CHAPTER 14

Obedience Is Better than Sacrifice

But Samuel replied: "Does the Lord delight in burnt offerings and sacrifices as much as in obeying the Lord? To obey is better than sacrifice, and to heed is better than the fat of rams." ~1 Samuel 15:22

As a parent, I want my kids to obey the first time. If I tell them to do something (or stop doing something), then I expect that they will comply. This tends to be very difficult for kids.

I have reasons for each command, whether it is, "Pick up your toys" or "Don't run into the street!" Most of the day-to-day instructions I give are intended to help them take care of themselves or treat others well.

Things like:

- Brush your teeth.
- Wash your hands.
- Stop hitting your brother. And ...
- Please stop putting dirty underwear in your brother's face! (Yes, I've had to say that one.)

Others may be life or death:

- Don't run in front of that car!

- Never shake the baby!

Everything I ask them to do, or not do, has a purpose: to protect them, to help them live a healthy life, to treat others well, to benefit them, or to live up to a standard I have for them.

At this point, since my kids are six, five, and under a year, their acts of disobedience are generally the same. Repeated. Over and over and over.

- Fighting/bickering with each other
- Not cleaning up after themselves
- Being disrespectful
- Not controlling their anger

It's easy to see a child's disobedience—it is usually pretty blatant and visible. My disobedience to the Lord tends to be ... more hidden, less obvious. Whether others can see it or not, it is there, cloaked behind my normal-looking life.

The things I tend to repeatedly struggle with are:

- Not making time to spend in the Word or in prayer
- Putting other things before Him, even if it is something good, like my family
- Not being active in love, not serving others or sharing my time

- Letting anger rule my heart, and being harsh with my children

These are just some examples. Really, is there any difference between my children's disobedience and my own? I repeat the same sins over and over. If you look at the Israelites in the Old Testament, they certainly make the same mistakes over and over. I say this to remind myself that we all have trouble with obedience, but why? Why is obeying so hard?

I thought about the answer, for myself, and two reasons came to mind:

1. For some reason, I think that God's way won't be good.

When I say it out loud, it sounds silly. But when I think about how I've held back from obeying, this seems to be at the root of it. When has God's plan not been the best for me? Have I ever regretted obeying the Lord? Nevertheless, my wayward heart lies to me and makes me think that my way is best. It's the oldest sin in the book.

2. I have to put my own desires aside.

When it comes down to obeying Him or not, the biggest reason boils down to ... I want what I want. Even though I know God's Word, and I know that He designed me, He can take care of me, and He has a plan for me, a little thing called pride gets in the way.

When I started thinking about the reasons my kids don't obey, I figured, *Why don't I just ask them?*

Their answers were:

- We're all sinners. (Really, that just sums it up.)
- I don't get to do the things I want to do, and it makes me mad.
- It's boring.
- I don't like it.
- It's hard.

Are their reasons any different from mine?

I remember one specific time I asked the boys to clean up their playroom. I went off and was doing something else and came back to check on them. There hadn't been much progress.

"What have you guys been doing?"

"Look, Mom! I made you a present!" said Gavin, my big-hearted four-year-old, with a grin.

"Gavin, I don't need you to build me Legos. I need you to obey and clean up. You haven't cleaned up at all."

It was in that moment I understood.

God does not need my "good works." He doesn't need me to give Him presents. He just wants me to obey Him.

I have thought about this one over and over, comparing this to my own life and my own disobediences. How many times have I tried to add on extra stuff, or meaningless tasks, when all I needed to do was obey? I know Gavin's heart was that he wanted to make me happy, but he had a skewed understanding of what I wanted from him. Is my view just as distorted?

Why should I obey God? I obey God because He loves me. I show God I love Him by obeying. When I put it that way, it changes my perspective. It makes me WANT to obey Him—not because I have to or just to follow a rule, but to tell God that I trust Him and His plan.

What is the result of obedience to God? I am living in Him. If I am living in Him, I have the fruits of the spirit—love, peace, joy, patience, kindness, goodness, self-control, faithfulness, and gentleness. I shine with Jesus.

What do others see? They see my actions and wonder, *Why?* I want to have the opportunity to explain to them who I follow and why. I want to give them hope.

But in your hearts revere Christ as Lord. Always be prepared to give an answer to everyone who asks you to give the reason for the hope that you have. But do this with gentleness and respect. ~1 Peter 3:15

If my kids happen to be obeying in public and are respectful to others, people notice.

"Your boys are so well behaved!"

It reflects well on us, as parents. (Granted, they do not see all the things that go on other times, but I accept the gracious comment.)

The same is true of me as a Christian. When I obey, I show others a true picture of Jesus. When I don't? I think that is evident in the popular opinion of Christians these days. I am seen as judgmental, hypocritical, unloving, and a bigot.

Whoever can be trusted with very little can also be trusted with much, and whoever is dishonest with very little will also be dishonest with much. ~Luke 16:10

As a parent, I am trusted with much. Leading by example and showing little hearts to Jesus are my most important missions. As a Christian, it is not any different. I am the picture of Jesus that people see. I am His hands and feet. May I hold myself to obeying God's standard, as I hold my children to obeying my own. And in that, I remember that the best way to show my love for God is to obey.

CHAPTER 15

Mama's Armor

Finally, be strong in the Lord and in his mighty power. Put on the full armor of God, so that you can take your stand against the devil's schemes. For our struggle is not against flesh and blood, but against the rulers, against the authorities, against the powers of this dark world and against the spiritual forces of evil in the heavenly realms. ~Ephesians 6:10-12

Here we sit, in the middle of spring break. For the last month, our home has been invaded by sickness. Winter decided to show up one last time before heading out this year and brought us cold weather and snow flurries. Because of the illnesses, we missed church two weeks in a row and almost a third (but we powered through and quarantined ourselves in the corner of the sanctuary).

There has been a lot of togetherness in this last month, with missing days of work, weekends spent recovering, and now, with Zachary in his first school spring break. It seems there have been some combative attitudes around the house as well, fighting with each other and testing every boundary.

All of these circumstances (I'm sure everyone has had times like these) have made us tired, whiney, yucky, and irritable. I feel exhausted and defeated, and I have a stinky attitude. My family is being attacked, and I have failed to suit up.

With a house full of boys, we have no shortage of superhero costumes. On any given day, you might see Darth Vader fighting Captain America. We have swords, shields, masks, capes, lightsabers, and blasters. Gavin's favorite superhero is Iron Man.

I feel like I could use that Iron Man suit right about now. I'd push a button and be protected head to toe, ready to defend and fight for my family.

I must remember that I am fighting FOR my family, and not against them.

One of my favorite people to follow and learn from is Brooke McGlothlin, author of *Praying for Boys* and co-founder of the No More Angry Moms of Boys Society (theMOBsociety.com).

In one of her programs, Fight like a Boy Mom (fightlikeaboymom.com), Brooke talks about fighting for your child, instead of against them.

When I went through this program a couple years ago, it impacted me significantly and changed my perspective and my approach as a mom. Don't get me wrong—I struggle every single day. But hearing what she had to say on this topic was truly life changing for me.

So when one of my boys gives me attitude and hurls mean words, I have to remember that I am fighting FOR their hearts, and not against them. I am fighting against the enemy who has come to kill, steal, and destroy.

Why now? Why do I feel so heavily attacked at this point in time? Never before have we all been sick for so long before. It feels personal. Why would the enemy be gunning for us right now? I thought about that and realized that everything really hit us after I decided to write this book. I knew that God had words for other parents out there. I chose to let God use me and my experiences to bring encouragement, support, joy, and hope to others who might be going through the same things.

As I sit here and write, I am pushing forward, knowing that there is a purpose for all of this. Sometimes you know you are on the right track when Satan tries to throw you off it.

Where have I failed, though? How can I withstand these attacks? What can I do to press forward with the plan God has for me?

I need to pull out my armor.

When I am struggling, when I am beaten down and weary, I need to go back and put on the Armor of God. I need to be Iron Mama. I need that suit to come out and protect every inch of me and give me the weapons I need to fight the enemy.

Therefore put on the full armor of God, so that when the day of evil comes, you may be able to stand your ground, and after you have done everything, to stand. Stand firm then, with the belt of truth buckled around your waist, with the breastplate of righteousness in place, and with your feet fitted with the readiness that comes from the gospel of peace. In addition to all this, take up the shield of faith, with which you can extinguish all the flaming arrows of the evil one. Take the helmet of salvation and the sword of the Spirit, which is the word of God. ~Ephesians 6:10-17

What does putting on the Armor of God look like?

The Belt of Truth – I don't listen to the lies of the enemy, the lies that tell me I'm worthless and I can't do this. I wrap myself in the truth of God's love. I surround myself in His plan for me. I share His truth with others.

The Breastplate of Righteousness – I protect my vital organs, my lifeblood, by putting on the Righteousness of Christ. I am not righteous, but the One who died for me is, and I cover myself in Him.

Feet Ready with the Gospel of Peace – I need to make sure I have my footing. I need to know where I stand, in the Gospel. I stand planted in His peace, ready and rested.

The Shield of Faith – I need to trust God and to know who He is. With this faith, I can block the attacks. I can stop attacks from piercing my heart when I know the God I serve is the One True God.

The Helmet of Salvation – I know from where my salvation comes—Jesus and only Jesus. I protect my thinking, I focus on my Savior, and I know I belong to Him.

The Sword of the Spirit, the Word of God – I need to arm myself with His Word. I must know it, say it, and live it.

I have been lacking in all of these areas. I've failed to pick up my sword. I forgot to buckle my belt. My shield is hanging, and my feet are tired. I have let the physical bring me down and misdirect me from the spiritual. I've let the lie creep in that hurtful words and attitudes from my children define me.

And pray in the Spirit on all occasions with all kinds of prayers and requests. With this in mind, be alert and always keep on praying for all the Lord's people. Pray also for me, that whenever I speak, words may be given me so that I will fearlessly make known the mystery of the gospel, for which I am an ambassador in chains. Pray that I may declare it fearlessly, as I should. ~Ephesians 6:18-20

If you are there with me, sword hanging and feet dragging, if you have done everything you can to stand, stand firm. Join me and sharpen your sword. Pick up your shield, and let's do this. I don't want to feel defeated, and I shouldn't! I am a child of the King! Sweet friends, let's not forget to arm ourselves and to lock arms with fellow fighters. I promise that you are not the only one. When you have done everything you can, rest in Him, and let that suit protect you from head to toe.

CHAPTER 16

This Little Light of Mine

You are the light of the world. A town built on a hill cannot be hidden. ~Matthew 5:14

It seems like when people know you have children, they want to talk about them, and most often, "they" are fellow parents. There is a camaraderie, a down-in-the-trenches commonality that we share. Maybe it is imparting wisdom, sympathizing with lack of sleep or sick kids, or laughing at the things kids say. It can happen anywhere, whether it's the office, school functions, or out at the grocery store, people are compelled to connect with you.

I have especially found this to be true when I have been pregnant. Looking back on it, I can see that MOST of the time, people have good intentions. They feel like they have this emotional connection to you because perhaps it reminds them of when they were pregnant or that they want to be pregnant, or maybe they just love babies.

Because I am no longer hormonal and carrying a child, I can now see that a little easier. However, especially when I was carrying Lincoln, I did not want anyone to speak to me—unless it was someone I truly considered a friend or a close family member. At work, I actually walked around with earbuds in ALL the time because I felt like I was a magnet for comments, over-disclosures, advice, and worst of all, plain rudeness. (Just for the record, it is never okay to tell a woman she looks like she is having twins or *triplets* or that she has gained weight. Seriously.)

I may not have had the best attitude by the time Lincoln finally arrived. (I'll ask for a pass for that time period, as he was a week past my due date.) But something others notice is my behavior toward my children—the way I talk to them, treat them, interact with them (showing patience, speaking kind words, standing firm in discipline)—those things all speak to who I am. It also speaks volumes to my children on how I value them. Those interactions, those words, will stay with them, whether I am tearing them down or building them up.

These are all perfect opportunities to share with others, the reason for my hope.

Therefore go and make disciples of all nations, baptizing them in the name of the Father and of the Son and of the Holy Spirit. ~Matthew 28:19

Being a light to my children has forced me to know why I believe what I believe. Just telling them about God has pushed me to dig deeper into my faith. Answering their questions has made me search and stretch myself.

I have three little witnesses to everything that I do, and I can tell you that they will call me on it. They see everything. I am more aware of my actions and what the boys are learning from them, even if I never say a word. They keep me accountable to live my faith each moment. It is painstaking work to lay the foundation of faith for my children. In the early days, it can feel fruitless and frustrating, but when the harvest comes, there is no joy like it.

Last summer (before Lincoln was born), when I was doing my normal bedtime routine with the boys, Zachary and I had been going over the story of the Crucifixion and Resurrection. He chose this story a lot and always said it was his favorite.

He had it memorized and liked to tell it to me. We had been having discussions about sin and what Jesus had done for us by dying on the cross, but it was not the first time we had talked about this. When it was time to say our nighttime prayer, he said he wanted to pray, but that he didn't want me to hear it.

"That's okay, Zachary. I don't have to hear your prayers. That is between you and God."

Pause.

"Well, I guess it's okay if you hear, Mom."

Zachary then proceeded to ask Jesus for forgiveness from his sins and to tell Him he wanted to follow Him and to be with Him in Heaven. My heart almost burst.

He was five and a half, so we wanted to be sure it was a genuine profession of faith and that he truly understood. He said he was scared to be baptized, so we waited for him to tell us he was ready. It took him about eight or nine months, but he finally said, "I'm ready to be baptized." We went over it with him again, and he was confident that he was a follower of Jesus. He spoke with our pastor, Coby, and we decided it was time.

Our church lets the child's dad actually baptize them, which makes it very personal and moving. I was a little concerned Zachary would be scared once he was up there, but we had been praying all week that God would make him brave. Stefan, shared a verse that his mother has always prayed over her children and grandchildren.

I have no greater joy than to hear that my children are walking in the truth. ~3 John 1:4

When Stefan asked Zachary if he wanted to follow Jesus, he shouted a resounding "Yes!"

Overflowing, pure joy swept over this mama.

One thing our pastor frequently tells us is, "Your kids are your number one mission field." If you are in the trenches, on the battlefield, fighting for your kids, be encouraged. I know it feels like they aren't listening, but they are. I know it seems like they don't see your actions, but they do. Stay the course, friends. There will be a harvest. It is worth it.

I want to be a light to not only my kids, but to as many as I can. This world is filled with so much darkness, and it is easy to let it overtake you. As you finish this book, know that I am praying for you. For you see, YOU are the reason I have written this book.

I pray that you are encouraged by these words. I hope that seeing my failures, victories, and experiences will help give you a new perspective. I pray you see God's heart and His love for you. I hope you realize your desire to know Jesus, and that you are not satisfied until you do. I pray you find joy and peace in Him.

Lord Jesus, hear my prayer for my friend.

I am not an expert—far from it. I am just a boy mom, sharing her heart. I have found I am moved most when others bare their souls. We need an honest, genuine, outpouring of the heart in order to stoke the flames of our own soul. I hope you are stirred, jolted into action, and into LIFE.

In His love,
Jodi

Urgent Plea!

Thank you for buying my book! I really appreciate all your feedback, and I love hearing what you have to say.

I need your input to make the next version better!

Please leave me a helpful REVIEW on Amazon!

Thanks so much!!

~Jodi

ABOUT THE AUTHOR

Jodi was raised out in the country in the Bootheel of Missouri, where farmland is prevalent and so is hospitality. She is the youngest of three, with two older brothers. Jodi played sports throughout her education and her first job was on a potato farm. She played outside, loved the open sky, and dreamed of creating something special someday.

Jodi grew up in the church but as she matured, she found herself searching for more. In high school she found a youth group where she discovered her desire to deepen her relationship with Jesus.

Jodi completed her education at Southwest Baptist University in Bolivar, Missouri obtaining her degree in Business Administration with a concentration in Marketing/Management. This is where she met Stefan and her heart was captivated. She dated him for five years and now they are about to celebrate their ten year anniversary.

Jodi is now a mama to three spirited boys who grow her faith and her heart daily. With rough-housing sessions in the living room floor and legos underfoot, Jodi finds refuge from the masculinity with her (girl) dog Gwynny. In a house full of boys you'd think Jodi would feel out of place, but she is happy and at home in the cuddly arms of her husband and sons. Jodi works full time in the banking industry and watches the St. Louis Cardinals in her remaining spare moments. She is active with her church family, teaching Sunday School and Vacation Bible School.

If you are interested in finding out more about Jodi, you can get to know her better through her blog "Mommy-hood Musings" at jodiarndt.com.

SELF-PUBLISHING SCHOOL

NOW IT'S YOUR TURN

Discover the EXACT 3-step blueprint you need to become a bestselling author in 3 months.

Self-Publishing School helped me, and now I want them to help you with this FREE VIDEO SERIES!

Even if you're busy, bad at writing, or don't know where to start, you CAN write a bestseller and build your best life.

With tools and experience across a variety of niches and professions,

Self-Publishing School is the <u>only</u> resource you need to
take your book to the finish line!

DON'T WAIT

Watch this FREE VIDEO SERIES now, and
Say "YES" to becoming a bestseller:

[https://xe172.isrefer.com/go/sps4fta-vts/bookbrosinc2565]

REFERENCES

All Scripture quotations, unless otherwise indicated, are taken from the Holy Bible, New International Version®, NIV®. Copyright ©1973, 1978, 1984, 2011 by Biblica, Inc.™ Used by permission of Zondervan. All rights reserved worldwide. www.zondervan.com The "NIV" and "New International Version" are trademarks registered in the United States Patent and Trademark Office by Biblica, Inc.™